Siberian Husky Puppy Training

The New Owner's Guide to Taking Care of and Training Your New Family Member

Mark Mathis

DISCLAIMER AND LEGAL NOTICE:

CONTENTS

WHY I WROTE THIS BOOK

I wrote this book out of my love for Siberian Huskies and the need for a beginner's guide to owning one. This is not one of those fill in the blank dog breed books that you see for sale online. This is truly a Siberian Husky only book and will always be. I will update this title from time to time as well as create more books in the future on other aspects of owning a Siberian Husky.

What this book is:

We want this book to be a resource for new owners on how to take care of and train their new Siberian Husky puppy by covering:

-History about your Siberian Husky you can tell friends and family about
-How to prepare your home for your Husky
-How to feed your Husky
-How to groom your Husky
-Teach your Husky basic training
-Learn your Husky's body language
-How to be prepared for emergencies

This book is for all of the Siberian Husky lovers out there.

You can find free training courses and updates on other titles at:

www.siberianhuskypuppytraining.com/newsletter

Thank You

SIBERIAN HUSKY HISTORY

Of course a quick look online will give you the history of this amazing breed but we threw a quick bit in here to make sure you get every ounce of information on your new dog. It doesn't hurt that it makes for an interesting conversation when someone asks you about your new puppy as well.

Origin
Siberian Huskies originated from the Northeastern part of Asia known as the Siberian Peninsula. For centuries, the local tribes of the Chukchi people depended on this hardworking breed for survival. They helped herd reindeer, pull sleds, and were able to work long hours in the freezing cold thanks to their thick coats.

Coming to America
Siberian Huskies were first introduced to America in 1908 when a Russian fur trader by the name of William Goosak imported a team of Siberians to Nome, Alaska for a sledding competition. Citizens of Nome referred to the smaller breed as "Siberian Rats" compared to their longer legged, and larger competitors. They came to finish third in the race while citizens of Nome rumored that gamblers bribed the driver to let the others win in fear of breaking the Bank of Nome following their 100 to 1 odds of winning.

The following year in 1909, after the breed showed their strength in the last race, a fellow competitor decided to import his own team of Siberians for the next race. He chose 60 of the best dogs he could find and imported them into Nome and formed three sled teams with them. Having two teams for his uncles and a team of his own, they hoped to dominate the race. Their teams placed 1st, 2nd, and 4th places when the race was finished. The winning sled dog team broke the previous time record for the annual 408 mile race by ten hours by finishing in 74 hours, 14 minutes, and 37 seconds.

The Nome Epidemic

Their next feat began in 1925 when Nome, Alaska was hit with a diphtheria epidemic. The closest serum that could save the town was 600 miles away. A dog sled team was formed to retrieve the medicine in Nulato 300 miles away. The team was driven by Leonhard Sappala with his lead dog Togo and knowing the urgency, he proceeded through Nulato and met the medicine on the eastern shore of Norton Sound. Even during a blizzard and after running all day, Sappala turned his team around and started heading back towards Golovin. There a rendezvous team driven by Gunnar Kaasen and led by Balto led the last leg of the trip to Nome saving the town. A statue of Balto stands in Central Park in New York City honoring the sled dogs of that day.

In 1926 after their brave actions in Nome, Sappala toured the country with his lead dog Togo. This was the first time the states were introduced to the Siberian Husky breed. When they arrived in New York City, Togo was awarded a medal by explorer Roald Amundsen, Sappala's former employer from a canceled expedition to the North Pole in 1914 because of World War I.

AKC Acceptance

The dogs that were first imported in 1908 by Goosak varied in size and weight. Some were shorter than others and some were symmetrically marked while others were not. Sappala while concerned about performance, began to breed Siberian Huskies to create a more uniformed standard. From his work, the breed was accepted and officially recognized by the American Kennel Club in 1930.

Their first standard was published in 1932 in the AKC Gazette.

IS A HUSKY RIGHT FOR YOU?

Huskies are a very sociable breed and love attention, meaning that if you cannot make a commitment to spend time with your puppy then a Siberian Husky is not meant for you. It would be best if you make arrangements for a family member to be home at all times. You can also provide companionship from another dog so they can feel like part of a pack.

Want a Guard Dog?

If you are looking for a guard dog, look elsewhere. Siberian Huskies are usually very friendly and docile, even to strangers. They may be more willing to lick an intruder in the face before stopping them or alarming you.

Activity Level

Siberian Huskies are extremely active dogs and need exercise daily. The best exercise would be running or swimming. You could use a harness and let them pull you on skates or a bike if they wish, they would have plenty of energy to do so. It's good to find mentally stimulating dog toys for them to use as well to keep them active and happy.

Ideal Climate

If you live in a warmer climate, make sure that you will be okay keeping your Siberian Husky indoors with you. Siberian Huskies were bred for the Arctic, never leave them outside in hot weather! Swimming can help alleviate the heat that your Husky may experience. Another note, **DO NOT** shave your Husky. Your Husky's fur works as an insulator against cold AND hot air.

Shedding

This leads to another point, if you have the need of living in a meticulously clean house then bringing home a Siberian Husky probably wouldn't be a good idea. Huskies shed a lot and are capable of being destructive if bored. Shedding can be minimized if you bathe and brush your Husky regularly.

Cleanliness

Siberian Huskies are also generally clean dogs. They like to keep their fur clean, so being indoors shouldn't be a problem for you. They don't like to make a mess when they eat and they do not have the typical dog odor people dislike.

Finding a Breeder and a Puppy

Contact your local animal shelters to find a good Siberian Husky needing a home. You never know where you will find your new best friend. The sites below can help you find one in your area.

www.adoptapet.com

www.petfinder.com

If you are dead set on a puppy, it's important to find a reputable Siberian Husky breeder in your area. Please avoid puppy mills at all costs. The American Kennel Club has a search function to find local Siberian Husky Breeders near you that they trust.

www.akc.com

Qualities of a good breeder:

- They will not sell puppies until they are at least 8 weeks old
- They will be there for support if you have any questions about your puppy
- They will provide registration papers and a purchase agreement
- They will take care of their dogs and puppies and you should be able to tell from their behavior with the dogs that they care for
- They will have a clean kennel or dog house premises and you will see healthy, happy dogs

Interview Questions

Before you even see any puppies from a breeder it's important to ask some questions about them first.

- How long have they been breeding?
- Are they a member of an AKC Parent Club or any related dog clubs?
- Do you have any references?
- Can you explain the breed's standard?
- May I see the older dogs on the property?
- What is the dog's temperament like?
- Do you show your dogs at dog show events?
- What health screenings if any have been performed on the parents?
- Do they have any documentation?

And most importantly ask yourself…

- Do I trust this person? Are they someone I would like to do business with?

THE SIBERIAN HUSKY BREED STANDARD

Height:
-Males usually measure from 21-23 1/2 inches at the withers.
-Females are usually smaller and measure from 20-22 inches at the withers.

Weight:
-Males are generally anywhere from 45 to 60 pounds.
-Females weigh a little less at 35 to 50 pounds

Colors
All colors from black to white are accepted as the standard along with red or brown. Siberian Huskies generally have white paws and legs with white marks on their face and tail as well.

Lifespan
You can expect your Siberian Husky to live an average of 12-14 years.

Coat
Siberian Huskies have a thick double layer coat of hair that was used to protect themselves from the harsh Arctic climate they were bred into to. The inner layer is dense and serves as insulation for heat and cold alike. Which is why you should NEVER shave a Husky. The outer coat has short straight hairs but are not as dense, they do however serve to help protect from dirt, water and other environmental elements.

Speed
Siberian Huskies are very high energy. Some people have trouble with their high energy level. A Siberian Husky puppy needs to be active almost the entire day. It needs a lot of exercise daily to stay happy. It only sleeps three or four hours at night. Be ready for some zoomies around your house if you do not keep your Husky wore out.

Husky dogs use this high energy to run quickly. In fact, Huskies are bred specifically to run. That's why if you own a Husky dog you should probably have a large back yard with a fence where it can run as much as it wants off its leash. The fence needs to be very high, because a Siberian can climb short fences easily.

How fast can a Siberian Husky run? The average Siberian Husky can run at top speeds of 28 miles per hour. He is not the fastest dog on earth, but he matches other dogs faster than him with his endurance level. Because of his high energy level, he can run fast for a very long time.

A Strong Animal

How much can a Siberian Husky pull? A good Siberian Husky can pull 25% of its own weight or more. In America, there are hiking contests to see what Husky can pull the most weight. A Husky pull with a team of Huskies can easily pull a man on a sled.

Siberians are mentally strong, too. They have been used in the military as search and rescue dogs, because they can withstand the extreme cold. They have also been used to haul supplies and gun parts to the troops.

Siberian Huskies need a lot of mental stimulation, and they are well-suited to many different kinds of sports. Urban mushing, scootering, flyball and hiking are just a few of the sports you can do with a Husky dog.

Huskies are extremely smart. They can be stubborn when you are trying to train them, but if you stand your ground, they can be a great service dog. The Siberian Husky is a great pet if you have a job for him to do. Just make sure you can keep up with him!

Choosing the Right Puppy

Picking out a puppy mainly boils down to their look and personality. You want a puppy that won't be too dominant to train and will look toward you as an Alpha leader.

While you are visiting the breeder take time to observe the litter and the behavior of the puppies together. You will begin to notice that some will be bossy, knocking others down and being noisy while others still are submissive to everyone and quiet. What you should be looking for are the puppies that are neither too bossy nor too quiet. They will be somewhat in the middle and thus easier to train.

PREPARING FOR YOUR PUPPY

Here is a checklist of things to have ready before your new puppy comes home.

Collars and leashes

You want to get a good sturdy leash and collar. Some Siberian Huskies do better with a harness. Using a collar will pull on their neck and some dogs have been found to think it's an act of aggression towards them. Siberian Huskies were bred to pull sleds by using a harness, it will be more secure and feel more comfortable to them. You also want a strong leash to go with the harness. You can try to find a matching color if you like, but it's more important to be the length that you desire and strong enough not to break. Make sure it's not too long that you have too much slack in the leash and have to roll it up. A good leash is usually around 5 or 6 feet long.

ID tags

This is very important, not only will tags display that your dog has been vaccinated but you want people to have a way of bringing your dog home if they are ever lost. With today's modern technology you can microchip your dog and all of your information will be found once the chip is scanned at a shelter or veterinarian's office. Be sure to ask your vet what is the most common chip brand in your area to be sure it can be read when your puppy is found. If you take good care of your Husky and train them well hopefully you will never have to go through the painful process of losing a family member.

Food and Water Dishes

Your puppy can't survive without food and water so be sure to get some quality bowls to supply them. Since your Husky will grow to be fairly large we recommend going ahead and getting food and water dishes with weighted bottoms so that as your puppy gets older he will not be able to dump them over and make a mess.

Pet Doors

Your Husky may love to run and exercise but they'll also want to cool off fast. So if you're inclined go ahead and buy a doggy door so they will be able to go in and out at their leisure.

Outdoor Kennel

You can keep them in an outside kennel while you perform yard work. Be sure to give them plenty of water, shade and keep an eye on that Houdini if you haven't escape proofed the kennel first. You never want to leave your Husky outside in the heat but they may enjoy the snow in the wintertime.

Grooming

We'll dedicate an entire section to grooming but for now you just need some hair scissors to help trim the hair on their paws, some nail clippers for dogs, a dog toothbrush, and a good fur comb such as the Furminator or something similar.

Dog Bed

Huskies love having comfy dog beds to hang out on while in the house. Go ahead and find a nice big one so they'll have plenty of room to lay out and relax instead of taking over your couch.

Fencing

Huskies are infamously known for their skill at escaping even the most secured areas. Be sure and get a good backyard fence that goes down beneath the soil. If you are able to pour a thin sheet of concrete a couple of feet deep around the fence as well that will help. It helps to give your Husky plenty of things to do in the back yard, Such as tunnels or a hill to sit up on. Having a sandpit will come in handy to prevent them from digging up your yard as well.

If you have to get a fence or if you have one already, make sure to check it for safety before letting your Husky play around it. This means that it's a t least 6 feet tall to help prevent your dog from jumping over it and check it for holes so your puppy can't squeeze through it at some point. It's also a good idea to bury plastic coated fence underground along the fence line to prevent your Husky from digging out. The plastic coating will prevent them from harming themselves. You can also pour a wall of concrete about two feet underground around the fence line and place concrete blocks around it to stop them from digging as well. If you have a fence with sharp pointed edges, your Husky could injure themselves on them so make sure they are removed or have been made safe.

Crate

The dog crate is an invaluable tool for house training. Using one will help assist in house breaking your Husky along with providing it a safe den for them to sleep. It's important to note that you should purchase a crate that will comfortably hold a grown Siberian Husky so that they can grow into it. Make sure that the crate is metal and not plastic. Plastic crates have been known to be chewed up easily and can injure your Husky.

Toys

Having plenty of toys is one of the most important things you can get for your Siberian Husky puppy. Aside from food and water of course. Huskies have an enormous amount of energy and it's important to give them exercise and keep them occupied every day. Besides the normal range of chew toys I'd advise you to go ahead and purchase a Kong. Kongs are useful as they can help prevent your Husky from getting bored from their meals. It keeps their mind stimulated as they try to get their meal out of the Kong. You can pack different layers of food "courses" into the toy allowing you to switch up the flavors and order of ingredients.

After buying all the necessary supplies and items it's time to prepare your home and make it safe.

CREATING A SAFE HAVEN

Kitchen
You want to be sure and put up any cleaners or chemicals that may be harmful to your dog along with a lockable trash can. Other than cleaners, be sure your family is educated on the types of foods that your Husky should not eat.

Foods that your Husky shouldn't eat:

- Caffeine - Anything with caffeine can be fatal to your puppy just stick to water.
- Chocolate - Same as caffeine.
- Alcohol - Just like humans, alcohol damages the livers of dogs as well.
- Avocado - The leaves, seeds and bark of Avocado contain Persin which is toxic to dogs.
- Macadamia Nuts - It takes less than a handful of these to kill your puppy, keep them away.
- Grapes or Raisins - If you eat these keep them put up far away from your puppy, they can cause kidney damage.
- Yeast Dough
- Raw or Under-cooked Meat (Educate yourself on raw diets before feeding your Husky raw meat. This is beyond the scope of this book but we may write one on the subject at a later time)
- Raw Eggs - Cooked eggs are fine and can provide extra protein but never feed raw eggs for fear of E. Coli or salmonella poisoning
- Small Bones - Never feed your puppy small bones that can be lodged in their digestive tract or choke on.
- Xylitol - This can be found in many gums and candies but can cause hypoglycemia in dogs.

- Onions - Damages blood cells and causes anemia.
- Garlic - Destroys blood cells just as onions do.
- Chives
- Milk - Causes diarrhea and dehydration, so no matter how long they give you puppy eyes for your ice cream just say no.
- Salt

Clean up the Bathroom

Be sure to have a trash can in the bathroom with a lockable lid to prevent them from diving into it. Keep all bathroom cleaners and bath soap away from you dog. Keep the toilet seat down to prevent your new puppy from drowning or any bacteria inside. All razors must be kept away from your puppy also. You can keep everything in a lockable cabinet if you must.

Bedrooms

Look around to be sure there are no jewelry, coins, hair ties, or anything else small enough to harm your puppy if they get it in their mouth. Check all the wires and make sure they are tied and put away to prevent your puppy from choking or electrocuting themselves.

Living Room

Again, check all of your cords and make sure they are neatly kept. Make sure you have no shoes, fake plants, books, magazines, remotes, or anything else you wouldn't want destroyed put away.

Home Office

If your home office is too cluttered to organize, (like mine...), just be sure to keep the door shut all times to prevent your Husky puppy from getting their paws on some paper clips, rubber bands, staples, letter openers, or any other supplies that they may find in there.

Garage

People's garages are normally filled with all sorts of poisons, such as antifreeze, paint, oil, gasoline, degreasers, fire ant killer or rodent poison among others. Be sure to keep your puppy away from this area unless you are escorting him to the car for a nice ride.

Backyard Safety

Make sure your puppy does not have access to any poisonous plants in your yard. We have a list of the most common poisonous plants in the emergencies section. Always roll up your hoses and put away any tools that your puppy may injure themselves, or choke on.

Swimming pools are a caution, always keep your puppy away from the pool until they are older. Swimming is great exercise for Siberian Huskies and helps them keep cool if you live in a warmer area. You don't want your puppy to fall in and drown though so be sure someone is always with them if you are teaching them how to use the pool.

THE FIRST WEEK HOME

Homecoming

When you go to pick up your puppy, bring a towel or spare blanket that you can rub on their mother and litter mates to help comfort your puppy with their scent on the first night in a strange place. Giving them a Kong toy with some frozen food inside to play with while he is in his crate will keep him occupied for a while. To prevent your puppy from crying at night you can cover their crate with a blanket which will help them feel secure. You can also try putting a mirror next to his crate to make him think he's not alone. Movies or TV shows with animals can help occupy and entertain them also.

Be patient and take the time needed to spend time with your new family addition, give them all the love and attention that they need. Go ahead and expect to take your puppy to the bathroom at last twice a night, they are small and have small bladders so well. It's a good rule of thumb to take them outside every hour or so.

Interacting with Your Puppy

When you get your puppy home go ahead and get them used to being touched all over, their ears, feet, legs, brushing their teeth, and touching their tail. This will help with the grooming process and help them feel safe while you clean them up. Always make sure to get in plenty of play time with your puppy to bond with them and become their best buddy.

Huskies and Children

Huskies are very friendly and are good with children. That being said though you still want to oversee any activity between children and your puppy to protect both parties from having an accident.

Huskies and Other Animals

If you have any other animals such as other dogs or cats, be sure and begin socializing the puppy with them as soon as they are comfortable. Huskies are prone to chasing and killing smaller animals but if you introduce them to your puppy as a pack member while they are young, they will learn to treat them as family in time. A good way to start is to place a barrier between them at first, such as a gate, just to make sure they can get along without harming each other.

Puppy Routine

It's important to go ahead and get your puppy into a routine that they can get accustomed to. A good one to use starts in the morning when you wake up:

1. Take your puppy outside to potty

Putting potty time on a schedule of when you wake up and then 2 - 4 hours after that teaches your puppy that they have a specific time to go to the bathroom and they can't just go whenever and wherever they feel like. Always reward your puppy for going outside. If an accident happens inside do not punish the puppy just clean it up when they are not looking. Be sure to use an enzyme cleaner such as lemon juice to erase any scent of the accident to help prevent it from happening again. By rewarding your Husky for using the bathroom outside, they will learn to go out if they want a reward. A good tip is to write down the time they go potty every time you take them outside so that you will know their bladder's schedule and can set an alarm to let you know it's time to take them out.

2. Feeding

Your puppy will need to be fed at least three times a day just like you until they are on adult dog food. Feed them first thing in the morning after taking them to go potty outside, then around noon and again around 5 or so. Take your puppy outside to potty after each feeding.

3. Training

You need to begin training your puppy as soon as possible the older they get, the harder it will be to teach them and get out of a habit. Go ahead and be teaching your puppy their name and words like "no", "bad", or "good". Start house training and teaching them to use chew toys instead of shoes or furniture as well. If you need help with the basics you can skip ahead to that section and come back later. You should strive to have your puppy well socialized with all animals by 5 months of age and completely house trained by six months. It's okay if they aren't yet just stay patient, keep working on it and they will get there.

4. Play and Exercise
Try to take two walks a day with your puppy or a good run once a day. You can start this after they are around 8 months so they are big enough to walk/ run with you. If you puppy is still young you can play with them in an enclosed area like your safe backyard you have already prepared. Walking and playing after eating will help create a habit in your puppy and they will get used to this daily routine.

Inside or Outside
You can surely keep your Husky indoors with you but I recommend training your puppy to go potty outside from day one. If you do not and begin to use puppy pads or newspapers they will begin to think they can go indoors and it will make it much harder to properly house train them. This brings us to crate training.

Learning to Love the Crate
Many new Siberian Husky owners look to crate training as a way to control their new puppy and keep it in check. This is fine, however as you prepare for dog crate training, be sure not to just throw the dog in a crate and leave. This will immediately create a negative association for the dog and a resentment for the crate. One of the best crates to buy is a 36" crate from Midwest Life Stages, it's easily fold able and has divider panels.

Start out early. Make sure the crate is set up when you bring your puppy home. Have the door open and a treat ready to go in the crate. Let the dog come and go as it pleases, praising the dog when it goes in, but not scolding when it comes out. Continue to encourage your puppy with treats to go in and out of the crate. At no point should you force the dog to go into the crate, this will only create negative associations.

It is also a good idea to establish a command for the dog early. Whenever it goes into the crate say something like "kennel up!" or maybe "go to your bed!" (Which is what I use with my dog.)

Shortly your dog will become comfortable with the crate. At this point you should begin to close the door for short periods, 10-15 minutes max at first. Don't leave the puppy, stay close by. The puppy will learn it can depend on you to let it out, creating an alpha bond with this knowledge.

Begin to work the dog into longer intervals, from 10 minutes, increase to 20 and then to 40 and so on, always praising the puppy for going into the crate, but never from leaving. Be sure that coming out of the crate is a neutral experience.

Finally, before leaving the dog for an extended period, make sure that your new puppy has played and exercised, gone to the bathroom and is tired. Initially leave the dog for an hour or so, then come back into the room. Don't let the dog out, just be seen. Then come back after two hours. At this point you may let the dog out. Keep this schedule for a day or two and soon your Siberian Husky puppy should be crate trained!

Time to See the Vet

According to the ASPCA the annual cost of care for a medium to large size dog runs from $620 to $780 a year. That being said you should always get your puppy spayed or neutered as soon as they are old enough which is generally six to nine months old. It helps them live healthier lives along with controlling the population of homeless animals. Get with your vet to determine a vaccination schedule as well.

Choose a Vet

Be sure to find a reputable veterinarian in your area. If you need to ask people you know who they recommend and go with the veterinarian whose name you hear the most. A good vet be willing to give you advice in any subject about your dog and take the time to educate you about your new family member.

The First Checkup

Ask your breeder about what kind of vaccination and worming schedule they use. You also want to find out what brands they trust and continue using those brand names. Do not mix treatments as this will make your puppy very sick. You also want to ask your veterinarian about which heart worm preventer they recommend.

How You Can Help Your Vet

When you are in the exam room, put down your phone and listen to your vet. This will show that you care for your puppy's well-being and are respectful. If your puppy is acting strange or have any abnormal behaviors from their usual do not be afraid to ask your vet about it. I know it's tempting to look online about your pet's symptoms and try to self-diagnose, but try to refrain from doing so and call a 24 hour veterinary service near you. Only a trained doctor will be able to recognize any symptoms and know what to do in an emergency.

FEEDING YOUR SIBERIAN HUSKY PUPPY

Nutritional Needs

Veterinary health professionals recommend that your dog requires the following nutrients:

- **12 Minerals** - Calcium, phosphorous, potassium, sodium, chloride, magnesium, copper, manganese, zinc, iodine, and selenium
- **11 Vitamins** - A, D, B1, B3, B5, B6, B12, Folic Acid, and Choline
- **10 Essential Amino Acids** - Arginine, histidine, isoleucine, leusine, lysine, methionine, along with phenylalanine, threonine, tryptophan, and valine
- **Fat** - Linoleic Acid
- **Omega 6 Fatty Acid**
- And of course plenty of **Protein**

Reading the Labels

Be sure to look at the nutrition labels of the food you feed your Husky. As you can see from the chart on the next page, it displays how much nutrients your Husky puppy needs compared to an adult Husky, it is crucial that you feed your puppy the nutrients their bodies require in order to grow strong and healthy.

Nutrient	Puppies	Adult Huskies
Protein (%)	22	18
Fat (%)	8	5
Calcium (%)	1	0.6
Phenylalanine (%)	0.89	0.73
Phosphorus (%)	0.8	0.5
Lysine (%)	0.77	0.63
Leucine (%)	0.72	0.59
Arginine (%)	0.62	0.51
Threonine (%)	0.58	0.48
Methionine (%)	0.53	0.43
Valine (%)	0.48	0.39
Isoleucine (%)	0.45	0.37
Chloride (%)	0.45	0.09
Sodium (%)	0.3	0.06
Histidine (%)	0.22	0.18
Tryptophan (%)	0.2	0.16

How Much to Feed a Siberian Husky

So what does a Siberian Husky eat anyway? How much do they eat? These are questions we'll be answering section.

Siberian Huskies are working dogs. This means that they require little food to function daily. Their specialized metabolism allows them to go for long periods of time without stuffing themselves. Recommended feedings are usually around 1.5 to 2 cups of food a day split between morning and evening meals. If you leave food out continuously however, you don't want to allow your Husky to overeat and become overweight. Overweight Huskies live a shorter lifespan and they will more than likely not be able to lose the weight. We recommend speaking with your breeder and/or veterinarian so they can recommend what they have been feeding their puppies and when you can switch to an adult dog food, which usually takes a year or two for your dog to become full grown.

What to Feed a Siberian Husky

We've found that professional sled dogs and show dogs do well from being fed 1/2 premium quality dog food and 1/2 raw meat such as beef, chicken or fish. Some tips to remember about raw foods includes:

- Do not leave meat out of the refrigerator for long periods
- Do not feed your dog smelly or green meat
- Make sure your dog is getting the right amount of minerals and nutrients in their diet
- Gradually move your dog to raw food meals
- Take notes on how they adjust to see if it's working well for them

If your Husky is just a domestic pet we don't recommend going raw unless you do your due diligence and perform research on creating a balanced diet for your Husky. This book does not cover raw diets.

The four most popular dog food brands that are nutritious and safe that have been recommended in no particular order are:

- Nutro
- Canidae
- Dr. Tim's All Life Stages
- Blue Buffalo Chicken

That being said you may have to experiment to find out which brand is easier on your dog's stomach. They may be from the same breed, but each dog is different.

Huskies are notorious at getting bored with their food, if this happens you can mince some raw chicken or fish to replace a 1/4 of the food they eat to give it a different flavor. You can also use a Kong to allow them to work for their food. By putting different layers of food inside the Kong, you can give your Husky entertainment and prevent them from being bored with the flavor as well.

The best thing to do would be to ask your breeder what they've been feeding your puppy and continue on that diet so as not to upset their digestive system. Your breeder should give you a diet sheet, and a short supply of the food they were using to give you time to get more yourself. If you have to change their diet, do so gradually so their digestive system can transition to the new food easily.

Some things that your Husky doesn't need to eat include:

- Cooked Bones
- Onions
- Raisins, prunes, or grapes
- Large amounts of dairy products (a small amount of cheese is fine if they are bored with their food)

GROOMING YOUR SIBERIAN HUSKY PUPPY

Your Siberian Husky will shed at least once but usually twice a year. It's good to get in a habit of grooming you dog daily or at least a few times a week. Brushing your Husky's hair will not only get rid of unwanted dead hair but also give you a chance to grow closer with them and get them used to a human's touch so they will behave if you or your veterinarian need to touch a sensitive area like their legs or in between their paws.

Brushing
Brushing your Husky can help build trust and be enjoyable for your puppy. As you get your puppy used to brushing you will find that they will start enjoying and looking forward to their brushing and bonding time with you. Huskies would groom each other out in the wild so brushing your puppy while they are laying down and submissive will naturally strengthen your role as the alpha in the house. Try to brush your puppy at least once a week if not more to keep that coat shiny and free of matted hair. Don't let your puppy's hair become matted from mud and snow as this will prevent the insulating properties of their fur.

Go ahead and take your handy dandy Furminator or another shedding specialty brush and brush your puppy in the same direction that their hair grows. Use short strokes in sections to be sure and get all of the hair out. Don't forget to brush under their belly, neck, and their tail. You finish using a softer brush with round teeth if you like. This will make your Husky love you even more from getting this special attention.

Shedding
At least once or twice a year your Husky will shed the under layer of their coat. This helps them in the warmer months to stay cool. Be sure to find a nice open area that will be easy to pick up all of the hair if you do not brush them outside. Huskies have been known to shed a lot, enough that you could probably use their hair to make a stuffed Husky plush! Of course you

always want to remember to NEVER shave a Husky. Their fur helps regulate temperature and if you shave your Husky not only are you ruining their coat but they could have a heat stroke and be burned from harmful UV rays coming from the sun.

Bathing

Huskies are a naturally clean dog, they like to keep themselves and their sleep area clean much like a cat would. You still want to bathe them a couple times a year at least but no more than once a month. If you bathe your Husky too much it could cause hot spots from them biting and itching dry skin. This will help get rid of unwanted hair that is falling out and keep your Husky feeling fresh. Whenever you find it difficult to help get the shedding hair out, give your Husky a warm bath and use a blow dryer to dry them while you brush them, this will help the hair come out easier. Make sure that the water is not too hot and will not harm your puppy, you want to clean them not burn them.

Ears

You want to keep your dog's ears clean as well. Never insert anything into your Huskies inner ears as this can harm them. Only use a dampened cloth or cotton ball to clean their outer ears and wipe them clean. If you have two Huskies or another dog, you may see them cleaning each other's ears.

Nails

If you can hear you Husky clicking through the house as they walk, their nails are too long and it's time for a trim. Hopefully you've been preparing for this by touching their feet and paws during brushing and bonding time. Start off gentle when you hold their paws to trim them. Be careful not to cut the nails too short and cause pain for your dog. A good way to tell where to cut is to look for where the pink color ends and cut a little after that area. This ensures that you will miss cutting any blood vessels and cause bleeding and pain. If you accidentally trim your Husky's nails too close to the quick and they begin to bleed, you can use Kwik Stop to stop the bleeding.

Teeth

It's a good habit to try and brush your dog's teeth everyday just as you would. Brushing their teeth will help fight off bad breath and give them healthy gums. While doing this check their gums for any discoloration or ulcers and bleeding. If you see anything unusual contact your veterinarian so they can treat it as soon as possible. To brush their teeth you must get them used to laying down on their side and being in a completely submissive position. If they don't like the idea of you using a toothbrush on their teeth you can start by using your fingers to apply the toothpaste using a finger brush and gradually moving to a dog toothbrush.

Professional Groomer

Grooming is definitely a lot of work to do but it's important that you perform the task yourself while they are a puppy and bonding to you. After they get older you can take them to a professional groomer once in a while where they can really get pampered. After they leave you'll be yelling "He's so fluffy!"

Fleas and Ticks

While you are grooming your Husky be sure and check them for fleas and ticks during the process. If you happen to see fleas, don't worry, you can simply use a fine-toothed flea comb to remove the vermin and dip them into a glass of hot water to kill them. If you a tick do not try to remove it with tweezers or your fingers. Doing so may cause the body to break off leaving the head in your Husky's body which could cause skin irritation leading to a visit to the clinic.

A PRIMER ON BASIC TRAINING

The Pack Mentality

One of the biggest challenges for owners of Siberian Huskies is dealing with the dog's "pack mentality". Huskies are pack dogs, with established hierarchy in their packs. Much like wolves they thrive in their pack and create bonds and show affection with the other members of the pack. As with any pack dog, this means that Huskies will always look for an Alpha when coming into a new home.

This alpha must be the owner. Huskies are perceptive dogs, and highly intelligent, but their need for an alpha must be met. If their owner cannot establish the alpha dominance, Huskies will quickly fill the alpha roll with themselves.

A common misconception of alpha behavior is that abuse or aggression must be used to communicate with the dog and this couldn't be further from the truth. Alpha behavior follows along the lines of respect more than strength. Be sure to not let your new puppy do whatever it wants. If it begins to jump on couches and furniture, firmly remove it. One common suggestion is to never feed the dog at the same time you eat, and certainly don't feed the dog from the table, make your dog wait until after you are done with your meal, then feed your dog.

Along these same lines, show your puppy affection at appropriate times. This may seem harsh at first, but soon the dog will understand that it must come to you for affection rather than being sought out for affection, a classic alpha behavior. Also be sure to establish yourself as alpha by always going through a doorway or passageway before the dog. Huskies respond well to these alpha cues, and will develop a bond of loyalty for the owner who can firmly establish themselves as alpha.

As always, consistency is key, do not falter or you may quickly find your dog had become alpha and you will have to work extra hard to take your position back. It's important to communicate this to your family so everyone can work together at training your dog.

After meeting with your family about the importance of the Alpha position, the next step will be setting training goals and agreeing on the same commands that you will use. It's important for everyone to use the same commands when training and commanding the dog so they will not become confused and will follow command.

A Not So Tight Leash

With Siberian Huskies exercise is paramount. They are active dogs, bred to pull sleds and as such they seem to be in a constant state of being ready to go. Owners of Siberian Huskies know that because of this regular activity is necessary in order to keep these dogs not only in good health, but in good humor as well. More than one horror story has been told of the Siberian Husky who became destructive, but the truth of the matter is that as long as your Husky is exercised regularly it will likely be friendly, docile and obedient.

Perhaps one of the best ways to exercise any dog is a regular walk and this makes leash training very important. Leash training a Husky so that it is not a fight to walk the dog every time can be a challenge. Remember, these are with dogs, bred to pull heavy loads over long distances. Their instinct is to pull, and they certainly will!

The first step to successful leash training is always being the dog accustomed to the collar. It would probably be ideal to use a harness rather than a neck collar, especially when training. Dogs view force or pressure on their neck as a sign of aggression, and may not take kindly to a subtle jerk or constant pressure from the leash.

Once your Husky is comfortable with its new collar, begin to attach the leash and walking the dog. Start in small areas, perhaps a living room or hallway. As the puppy masters obedience in smaller areas, move to something bigger, the backyard perhaps, then around the block before finally opening the world up to your puppy. To prevent forming arthritis it's important that you only walk your puppy for five minutes per each month of their age. For instance if your puppy is six months old, only walk them for 30 minutes. After their joints stop growing at around 14 to 16 months of age you can rest easy knowing they can run as much as they want.

A very popular way to initially train your puppy is a basic red-light/green-light method. When the leash is taut, don't move. Get the dog to sit, or stop moving before walking again, but always make sure that the leash is slack before moving again. Be consistent in this though, Huskies are intelligent and perceptive and will take inconsistency as cues to encourage improper behavior. Don't forget to praise the good behavior! Do not jerk the collar or put lots of pressure on the dog either, though collar corrections may be necessary. These are short, well timed tugs on the leash to correct your dog's course. Don't pull so hard that the Husky will view it as aggression, just short bursts when the dog begins to wander to keep it on course.

Keep your puppy on a short leash throughout the process. Don't give the puppy free reign to go wherever it wants, keep it by your side and walk slowly and purposefully. Before long you will find that through your consistency and perseverance you Siberian Husky puppy will be happy and willing to be on its leash!

Prepare for Treats Training

You want to be sure and keep a variety of treats for your Husky due to them getting bored from the same food easily. So grab you a treat bag and prepare some treats for your Husky. Some good ideas include:

- Cut up steak
- Some dry kibble
- Soft treats
- Small balls of cheese

When cutting up your meat treats, be sure to cut them to about the size of a pencil eraser. This will make the meat last longer and be quicker for your Husky to eat. A good trick is to keep a mixture of these in your treat bag to keep your Husky guessing. You can look in our resources section for a list of treats we recommend.

BASIC TRAINING COMMANDS

Here are some basic every day commands that you will commonly use with a Husky. Be sure and practice them every day and in different ways with different treats so that your Husky doesn't become bored.

Name
The first thing you want to teach your puppy is to learn their name of course.
- You can start by saying their name until they give you their attention with eye contact then immediately give them a treat and praise them.
- Try practicing while you sit or lay down and at random times. You want to practice this everywhere and as much as possible until they will give you eye contact without needing a treat.

Come
Teaching the command come would be the next logical step in order to stop your puppy from chasing something they shouldn't be or trying to run off if you accidentally drop your leash.
- Put a collar and leash on your Husky.
- Drop down to their level and say "come" while pulling on the leash. When they get to you reward them with a treat and your praise.
- Once they get used to this action, start trying it without a collar and in an enclosed area. You can start to increase the distance between you gradually, but always practice this trick in a safe enclosed area with a high fence.
- Never let your Husky get off leash in the open. Even the most trained Huskies have been known to run off when taken off the leash and get injured or worse. You do not want to experience that kind of pain, better safe than sorry.

Sit

Teaching your Husky the sit command is useful when you want them to calm down and focus on you for another command. To teach this simple command:

- Hold a treat near your Husky's nose.
- Start moving your hand upwards and over his head causing him to follow your hand while their bottom lowers.
- Once they are sitting down, say "sit", give them the treat and show them praise.
- You'll want to repeat this a few times until your Husky is capable of doing it without following your hand or seeing a treat.

Stay

After your Husky masters the sit command, stay would be the next command to teach in order to keep them waiting on you.

- Give your Husky the command to sit.
- After they sit down hold your hand up and say stay, then slowly take a few steps back away from them.
- If they stay, even if it's only a few seconds, return to them and reward them with a treat and praise.
- Every time you practice, try moving further and further away as long as they stay put. Do not reward them if they come all the way to you.
- If they move simply bring them back to their sitting position and try again, maybe while moving back slower.

Drop It

This command is an important one if you want to save your shoes from being destroyed one day. Puppies will put anything into their mouths they see and it may be critical one day to get them to drop whatever valuable they have found so you can save it. The way to teach this is to basically bribe your Husky puppy with something better than what is in his mouth.

- Grab your good treats and find some of your Husky's favorite toys to practice with.
- Get your Husky to start playing with one of their favorite toys.
- While it is in their mouth show them the treat and say "drop it".
- When they open their mouth for the treat reward them and pick up their toy.
- Keep practicing this until they can follow the command without seeing a treat.
- If they ignore their toy because they know you have treats that is fine, simply do it a random times throughout the day to throw them off.

You want to keep practicing this command while increasing the quality of the item they have in their mouth. Once they master it try practicing outside as well where there are many more distractions.

Leave it

Huskies are curious creatures, so teaching your Husky the "leave it" command could be an important one for you. For instance, you may catch them starting to dig in your favorite flower bed and want them to stop immediately...

- For now put a treat in both of your hands and close your fists, make sure the one that is rewarding has a better treat than the decoy.
- Let your Husky sniff at one of your enclosed hands. Allow them to sniff or lick at it but ignore them.
- Once they stop trying to get to it, reward them from the other hand with a treat.
- After they master this skill it's time to move on to using an open hand. If they try to get the treat out of the open hand close it again.
- Do this until they ignore your hand and the treat and then reward them from the other hand.
- The next phase will be placing a treat on the floor and covering it with your hand.
- Once they are done trying to get it reward them from your other hand like before.
- When they can ignore the treat after your "leave it" command, you can place the treat on the floor and gradually start to raise your hand over it, but covering it if they try to get it.
- If they can leave the treat alone while your hand is around six inches away from it start teaching "leave it" while standing up.
- Only reward your Husky if they ignore the treat on the floor. Once they master this you can use the same technique to start practicing with other objects, animals or people.

Formal Obedience Training

If you want professional help seek out an obedience training school or class in your local community. Not only will they assist you in your training but it will be a great place to socialize your Husky with other dogs as well.

You can find free training courses and updates on other titles at:

www.siberianhuskypuppytraining.com/newsletter

WHAT IS YOUR SIBERIAN HUSKY PUPPY TRYING TO TELL YOU?

Since your Siberian Husky puppy can't speak to you it's important to know their body language. You can learn a lot about what your Husky is feeling or thinking simply by observing how they move.

Bowing

If you catch your Husky bowing down at you with their tail wagging then they are telling you they are ready to play. So grab a toy and go have fun!

Nudging you

If your Husky nudges or hits you with their nose, they are trying to get you to play with them. Where bowing would be asking for you to play nudging is their way of demanding your attention. Huskies that are more dominant than others are likely to do this.

Holding your hand

To show their affection for you, your Husky may try to hold your hand in their mouth. This is an important bonding activity that you should take part in as it's their way of telling you to trust them and that they will not bite you.

Licking or Biting

Be sure to keep an eye out for this. If they are simply licking or biting the base of their tail they could have fleas. If they continue doing so for prolonged periods of time however, it could be a compulsive behavior. Be sure and speak to your veterinarian on treatment so your Husky will not begin to get raw or bleed from those areas.

Head tilting

This is a universal sign for a curious or puzzled dog. With Huskies being naturally curious animals, you may see this a lot, unless they are sick and are showing other symptoms.

Sniffing or circling

This is how all dogs greet each other they may start at one end and work their way to the other. You may catch them sniffing humans as well.

Mounting

If your Husky is trying to mount another dog or a human, it is usually more of a dominant behavior. That is their way of showing their power over others. If you have done your job of becoming the pack leader you shouldn't have to worry about this.

Pawing

Your Husky may try to place their paw over the shoulder of other dogs in an effort to establish dominance over them. They will also do this by placing their chin over other dogs.

Tail

You can learn a lot from your Husky simply by observing their tail. They will usually leave their tail down and keep it relaxed. If you see them curl up their tail then they are excited, when they wag their tail it's the same as if they are smiling or could also be nervousness depending on the situation. If their tail is erect and has a shorter arc it may be a sign of dominant aggression. If they hold their tail between their legs than they are being submissive or fearful.

Sleeping style

Paying attention to how your Husky sleeps can also give you a clue to how they are feeling. For instance if your Husky is cold they may curl up and use their tail to cover their nose keeping it warm. This is commonly called the Siberian Swirl.

If you see your Husky yawning they may not exactly be tired. Yawns can also indicate tension or anxiety. You can watch your Husky before a walk or ride in the car to see if they are feeling anxious about anything and help them feel relaxed.

If you find your Husky snuggled up close to you, they're probably not trying to keep warm as their bodies are warmer than yours. Most likely they're trying to feel safe in your presence. If they are more of an alpha dog they may keep a little more distant from you signifying that they like feeling secure but can protect themselves. Of course the less dominant your Husky is the closer they may sleep near you.

You may find your Husky lying flat on their stomach with their legs spread out. Don't worry they're just hot and trying to dissipate their body heat. If you find your Husky sleeping on their back with their legs in the air, then you can rest easy as well because you have a happy, care free and self-assured dog. Your Husky puppy experiences (REM) or rapid eye movement just like humans do. Do not disturb your Husky while they are dreaming as they could be experiencing a nightmare. Even the calmest dog can snap at you if you wake them at the wrong time.

Recognizing pain

Your Husky will try hard to hide their pain, but it's your job as their owner to recognize signs of pain in order to help them feel better. Even the slightest difference in their walk could signify something is wrong so be sure and pay attention to your Siberian Husky puppy.

You can use this list of symptoms to determine if you need to take your Husky to your vet immediately for help.

- A loss of appetite
- Favoring a specific part of the body
- The sight of blood on your Husky or the floor
- Any kind of swelling
- Acting more aggressive or more timid
- Not wanting to exercise or play
- Having trouble going up or down steps
- Stumbling
- Acting lethargic

EMERGENCY PREPAREDNESS

Here we include a list of certain emergencies for you to be prepared for in case your Siberian Husky is in a life threatening situation.

First aid kit
You want to make sure that you're prepared for any emergency situation that arises in case your Husky gets hurt. You could easily keep these items in a case for storage and easy travel.

- Blanket or towel: not only will it keep them warm, but you can also use it to wrap them up and carry them to an emergency clinic.
- Muzzle: even the gentlest dog has been known to snap when they are in pain. This will keep everyone safe.
- Tick remover: Using a kit such as Ticked Off, makes it easier to remove ticks from your Husky without leaving the head in the skin causing irritation.
- Canine rectal thermometer: Use with Vaseline or another type of lubricant. The normal temperature for a dog is 99.5-102.5 Fahrenheit. If you see the temperature reading above normal that is a red flag, and the dog should be taken to your emergency animal clinic as soon as possible. A body temperature of at least 103.5 degrees Fahrenheit can be considered a fever.
- Hydrogen peroxide: You can use this as a disinfectant as well as a way to induce vomiting if your Husky has swallowed something poisonous. To induce vomiting it takes 1 to 3 teaspoons every 10 minutes until they vomit. Always check with you vet before you induce vomiting because the situation may cause for something else.
- Tweezers: Use these to remove bee stingers, splinters, thorns etc.
- Kwik Stop: You can find this in your local pet store. It's used if you

accidentally trim your Husky's nails too close to the quick and it begins to bleed. You can their nails with this powder to stop the bleeding. If you don't have time to get Kwik Stop you can use flour.

- Gauze and tape: Have a roll of gauze handy, along with pads about 4"x4" and bandage tape to hold it all together.
- Antiseptic ointment: Use something like Neosporin to help any cuts heal and prevent infection.
- Exam gloves (nitrile, latex, or rubber): Use these to prevent spreading infection to yourself or others in your household.

Some other useful items would include:

- Ace bandage
- Activated charcoal
- Alcohol prep pads
- Cold pack
- Cotton balls and Q-tips
- Ear and oral syringe
- Epsom salts
- Eyewash
- Imodium A-D (1 milligram per 15 pounds, once or twice daily)
- Kaopectate (1 milliliter per 1 pound every 2 hours)
- Magnifying glass
- Milk of magnesia, antacid and laxative
- Mineral oil, laxative (5 to 30 milliliters per day)
- Providone-iodine ointment
- Rubbing alcohol
- Scissors (small blunt-end type)
- Splints

Medications

Some useful over the counter medications include:

- Aspirin comes in 81mg and 325mg. A usual dose for dogs is about 5mg per pound every 12 hours. Do not give a dose more than twice a day until you talk to your veterinarian.
- Benadryl comes in a 25mg capsule or tablet. This can be helpful for dogs with allergies or for reactions to insect bites. In this case the dose is 25mg per 25 pounds, can be given every 8 hours up to a maximum dose of 3 times a day. There can be some abnormal reactions that

include sedation or in rare cases, intense excitability.

- Pepto-Bismol may be given to your Husky if they have diarrhea by administering one dose of 1 teaspoon per 5 pounds every six hours. Be informed that this may cause dark shaded stools, don't worry however as this is harmless.
- Hydro cortisone cream can be useful for treating irritation from insect bites, itchy skin or allergic reactions.

If you are unable to get to a vet immediately here are a couple of 24-hour emergency numbers staffed with experienced veterinarians:

ASPCA Animal Poison Control Center 1-888-4-ANI-HELP or 1-888-426-4435

National Animal Poison Control Center 1-800-548-2423

Snake bites
Snake bites are serious business. Not only does your Husky have a higher chance of being bit by playing in the outdoors but they have a higher chance of dying from them as well.
If your Husky is bitten by a snake:

- Always assume it was a venomous snake.
- Get your Husky to your vet immediately.
- If your dog's face is swelling, avoid touching it all together.
- Immobilize the part of your pet that has been bitten, if you can do this safely. Try to keep the bitten area at or below the level of the heart to keep the poison away.
- If you can't keep your Husky immobile and calm during transport, carry them instead.
- (Side note: Snake bites are severely painful, the swelling that can occur will happen quickly and may shock you. Due to the pain your Husky can be fearful and may unwittingly try to snap at you.)
- What you shouldn't do:
- Never try to draw out the venom.
- Never cut open the area around the bite (you will only wound your Husky).
- Never use a Snake Bite Kit they can actually cause more harm than good.
- Never apply cold packs or ice to the wound, doing so will cause the blood vessels constrict around the area and concentrate the venom

causing serious muscle damage to the constricted area.

- Never rub any ointment into the bite, the venom is in your Husky's blood stream, so anything topical is useless.
- Never apply a tourniquet as this could cause further tissue damage, it could also cause the need for limb amputation.
- Never allow your Husky to move about freely, keep them still.
- Tips to prevent snake bites
- Stay on open paths while hiking with your Husky.
- Stay away from dense or high grass and rocks with holes where sneaky snakes like to hide.
- Don't let your pet inspect holes or dig underneath rocks.
- If using a tie out lead, check that the whole running area is not inhabited by snakes.
- Remember that a snake can only strike from a distance of half its body length. Give the snake time to go away, they don't want to approach you or your Husky if they can help it.
- Don't let your Husky get near a lifeless snake as they still can release venom.

Bleeding

If you find your Husky bleeding, you follow first aid procedures immediately. Place a gauze pad over the wound and apply pressure until the bleeding stops. You can use your bandage wrap to hold it in place if you need to. If bleeding does not stop take your Husky to the vet immediately. If in a life and death situation, you may need to tie a tourniquet between the wound and your Husky's heart. Only use a tourniquet in a life and death situation as it can be dangerous for your Husky and cause for them to have a limb amputated.

Fractures

If your Husky has suffered a fracture, you need to keep it immobilized to prevent them from being injured further. To keep their leg immobilized, place to sticks on either side of their leg for support and wrap over them with towels or magazines to hold them in place as you rush to the vet clinic.

Heat stress

Your Husky's normal resting temperature is around 100.5 to 102.5 degrees Fahrenheit. If their temperature exceeds 105 degrees, changes begin to take place in their body to try to cope with it leading to heat stroke.

Some symptoms of heatstroke include:

- Uncontrollable panting
- Vomiting or Retching
- Lethargy
- Collapsing
- Large red gums
- Thickened saliva
- If your Husky starts to show these symptoms after being in the heat outside you need to follow these procedures as soon as possible:
- Get them into the shade.
- Use cool water, not ice water from a hose or faucet to wet their foot pads, stomach and inner thighs.
- Do not place your dog into a pool or bathtub. If you do, it could cool them down too rapidly and can lead to cardiac arrest or bloating.
- Do not cover your Husky with a towel or blanket. This could lead to creating a sauna effect making things worse. Do not place them in a kennel or any other enclosed area. Keeping them in any open area with good air flow is ideal for helping them cool down. Letting them sit in your car with the air conditioner blowing on them is a great option.
- Keep them moving. Try to keep them walking around slowly to let their cooled blood circulate the body. If they lay down then blood may pool up in certain areas and not help in the cooling process.
- Let your Husky drink small amounts of water. Do not allow your Husky to gulp down water, drinking cool water too fast can lead to them bloating or vomiting. It's best to allow them small amounts that are cool but not ice cold.
- Do not give your Husky human energy or performance drinks. Energy and performance drinks were not made for canine consumption and could harm your Husky. If they will not drink any water you can try feeding them some cool beef-based broths or maybe some chicken.

Poisonous Plants
Please keep these poisonous plants away from your Husky to prevent them from harming themselves while looking for a chew toy.
- Amaryllis
- Autumn Crocus
- Azalea
- Castor Bean
- Chrysanthemum

- Cyclamen
- English Ivy
- Iris
- Kalanchoe
- Lilies
- Marijuana
- Mustards
- Narcissus bulbs
- Oleander
- Peace Lily
- Potatoes
- Pothos
- Rhododendron
- Sago Palm
- Schefflera
- Tulip
- Wild Radish
- Yew

Symptoms of poisoning:

If your Husky is experiencing any of these symptoms please get in touch with your emergency veterinarian for help immediately.

- Dilated pupils
- Vomiting and/or diarrhea
- Irritation near their mouth
- Swelling of their mouth or throat
- Uncontrolled drooling
- Uncontrolled thirst
- Inconsistent heartbeat or breathing
- Muscle twitching
- Seizures
- Coma
- Death

Porcupine quills

If your curious Husky has gotten himself into some trouble with porcupines, you should take your dog to the vet as soon as possible. Your vet will be able to pull the quills out quickly and easily while your Husky is under anesthesia. You should minimize the movement of your Husky, if there are quills near the legs or chest they can migrate further into their body, puncture organs and in worse case scenarios, cause death.

CONCLUSION AND THANK YOU FOR READING

Thank you for reading this guide. I hope it helped answer any questions about owning a Husky puppy and set you in the right path of a happy relationship with your new family member.

Join our Facebook Group to share your experiences and tips with our fellow community members.

https://www.facebook.com/groups/huskypuppytraining/

Printed in Great Britain
by Amazon